River by the Glass

River by the Glass

Monika Rose

Manzanita Writers Press • San Andreas • California

Copyright © 2011 by Monika Rose. All rights reserved. Printed in the United States of America. No part of this book may be used or reproduced in any manner without written permission. Reprinted 2022

Publisher: Manzanita Writers Press
manzapress.com
manzanitawp@gmail.com
PO Box 215, San Andreas, CA 95249

ISBN: 978-1-952314-04-9
Library of Congress Control Number: 2010926429

For copies or permission to reproduce selections, contact author:

Monika Rose
PO Box 632
San Andreas, California 95249
E-mail: mrosemanza@jps.net
Website: monikarosewriter.com

Cover Photo Front: *Clavey Sunburst*
Cover Photo Back: *Waterfall, Clavey River*
Cover Design and Layout: Joyce Dedini
Author Photo Copyright © 2005 Björn Kesting
Photography Copyright © 2011 Ron Pickup. The photographs in this collection are black and white renditions of color images taken from photography exhibitions—*On the Stanislaus: A Stream of Life*, and *The Clavey, A River Running Wild*, by Ron Pickup.

For Gary

Introduction

I first published Monika Rose's poetry in the *Mindprint Review*, a literary journal of regional and international writing and art published back in the late 1980s. And even then, I was taken with her whimsical wit and metaphysical humor in poems such as *Carp* and *Eye*.

Today, she has evolved these skills into the biting imagery but sensitive and haunting verse found in the likes of *Drowning at the Kern*, *Chester and the Bluebird* and *On the Fence*. This is the ethereal yet concrete fine poetry of a master poet.

In *Chester and the Bluebird*, a spirited blue bird standing in for a beloved pet steer, just reduced to sizzling steaks on the family barbecue, is Rose's respectful reply to the classic, important image of a *red wheel / barrow / glazed with rain / water / beside the white / chickens,* written by the pillar of Objectivism, William Carlos Williams.

The poetry in this collection has been forged and tempered over decades of writing, while also teaching English at the secondary and college level; attending numerous workshops with some of the best writers of our time; and promoting and showcasing the work of her fellow writers and artists through founding Writers Unlimited and editing and publishing the *Manzanita* anthologies and other publications.

With the publication of *River by the Glass*, we at last have the collected poetry to date of the hardest working poet I have been privileged to know.

> Ron Pickup
> March 23, 2011
> Soulsbyville, California

Contents

I—Drowning at the Kern

Drowning at the Kern   15
Cleaning Fish   18
Carp   20
Variations on a Skipping Stone   22
Obsidian   23
Tuolumne River   24
What I meant to say was   28
Folk Tale   29
River by the Glass   30
The Fish   32

II—On the Fence

On the Fence   37
Marimba Mountains   41
What Is to Wilderness   42
Chester and the Bluebird   44
Deer in the Road   48
Fragment   50
Animal, Vegetable   51
Four Levels of Mist   52
Auto Archeology   54
Mouse Leaves   56
Nails   58
Bull Pine in the Window   60
Solitude   62
Sound Barrier   63

III—Mirror

Mirror   67
Slow-pitch Poetry   68

Life of Letters   70
Eye Think   72
Drop of Moon   74
A Poet   76
Alignment   78
Glass   80
Transcendental Perch   81
Eye   86
Love and Finance   88
Beauty and the Beast: The Movie   90

IV—From the Other Side

From the Other Side   97
Black Dog   100
Fire Safe   102
Returning from Iraq   103
Need Fire   104
Haiku-Like   106
Battered Woman   108
Food for Thought   110
Leper Lady at Swiss Park   111
Navajo Traveler   112
Piercing   116
Tuolumne Meadows Bridge   118

V—The Long Dance

The Long Dance   123
Song for Sisters   126
There is a Cough   128
What Yeats Knew   130
Father   132
The Ritual of Coffee Making   134
Bull Pine   135

A Living   136
Photo Album Leaves   138
Moon Predictions   140
Navajo Gifts   142
Desert Bloom   144
Coming into Love   146
Accidents of Moon   148

VI—You *Can* Take It With You

You *Can* Take It With You   153
Worms   158
Estate Sale   161
Top of the Mountain   164
How to Spot a Serial Killer   168
Venial Sin   170
Yellow the Dead Canary   172
Yoga at the Y   174
To the Core   176
Passing Time   177
Amoura   178

VII—Eye for an Eye

Eye for an Eye   183
Milk   184
Gift of the Fat Dalmatian   186
After the Fall   188
Back to Back   190
View of the Garden by a Visitor   193
Gold in the Cracks   196
Parthenogenesis   198
Space   200
Harmonica   202
Lizard   203

Falling Water, Tuolumne River

I

Drowning at the Kern

*...but we wish the river had another shore,
some further range of delectable mountains.*

—Robert Lowell

Drowning at the Kern

Trout expose themselves
Flippant silver streaks
White water turns
A slow blue

Quiet comes to the river as
Mudsuckers in two-foot pools
Turn and turn uneasily

      Will—iam!
           Will—iam!

The river trickles to a halt from
The shutoff above
Exposes the crying
Of a woman
Waist deep in her rival

      Will—iam!
           Will—iam!

She drags towards shore
Her feet stones
Blue clothes cling like wet plants
Hair snags her shoulders
In algaed strands

           Will—iam!

Her arms drip
Body pulls down
Trying to root

She rolls into a ball on the sand
Head down in her legs
She curls into herself, alive
Her feet stick out
Large and white

Fish swim in shallow pools
Slowly visible, think water is
Still marble, hiding their moves

Divers drag William out of the river
Cover him with blankets and shiver

The bottoms of his flat
Feet glisten frozen
Like ghost trout suddenly
Splitting the surface

The woman unravels herself
And flops onto what was once love
They try to peel her away
And she fights them to stay

    Will—iam!

They were married just yesterday
Someone whispers what a shame
Willows rustle and wind shifts screes
While a mouse skitters among the leaves

River starts to rise
Exposes shoulders
Of boulders and banks and
Covers what once was. What once is.

Cleaning Fish

Take a fish any fish
Let's say a black bass

Or iridescent rainbow
Trout after it has

Stopped flopping
In the sink

Its dull eye fixed
On an isolated splash

Before it slips down
Into darker water

Slimy silver moons
Weigh in, light-heavy

Take what remains of slippery
And hold it still

Under the blade while some
Scales flip into the drink

And others fly free
As if to attach again

Why not hold a side to start
And pinpoint where guts reside

Then plant the knife tip for a slit
As a slant hand slips a bit

The one eye squeeze
And shut will sharpen

A drain of senses
And ooze of essence as

The next step
Is not so clean

Carp

Ukranian fisherman
fish for carp
aghgh

American don't know
what is good
they don't eat carp
too many bones
too lazy

Canadian like carp
you know
by truck full
carp cutlets
smoked carp
pickled carp
carp ground bones
and ever-ting

You fishink for bass ?
using lures?
naagh
won't catch nottink
you know
too warm here
too shallow here
you fish for carp

Come I show you how
use corn meal balls
like this see?
now watch okay
(his teeth are squared down to
half size like he was raised
eating rocks)

Aghgh
carp is good
American don't know
what is good.

Variations on a Skipping Stone

I found a perfect skipping stone
And waited for a perfect time

Found a perfect skipping stone
And wind convinced me otherwise

Found a faulty skipping stone
And it skipped me countless times

Found a perfect skipping stone
And threw it perfectly wrong

Never found a skipping stone
That yearned for water

Obsidian

Black pond of my heart
Expose no stone

Shine honest
And clear to me

Reveal your soul
Reveal nothing

You are cut water
Before corruption.

Tuolumne River

The river spreads her hips
ready for winter birth of waters
waiting for the break, a flood

Now August in her dry time
birthing channels ready
granite pelvis arches

She eddies and rests
waits for the first flash
of conception

When one early storm's
caresses will urge and
certainly take

My own river runs past fall
as a trickle hints that
my flow moves beyond me

To tributaries spawned in their own spring
two daughters of swirling mist,
and a gathering storm of son
press out their own streams

The family astrologist gushed years ago:
Abundant water signs reflect
at least ten children in your picture
watch your uterus

And I did, then closed my eyes
and launched
a flow of three

Who leapt out in the salmon way
from a source beyond me,
rivulets of new century,
cleansing effluvial fans

That waved the easy rush
of sensual water meeting water,
and a quiet concussion.

I almost lost them
to the Mokelumne River
at flood stage one spring

But they swam back
to tip the scales in favor
of always leaving

When my son sprang
from the womb
gasping, his gills gone

Yowling in fluorescent
light, gulping in
conditioned air

He coughed up my brine
and swam in his own stream
of secret percussion

The middle one waited
in shallows fin deep
for a sign to join the light

At a signal, the flip of fish
surfacing briefly for the fly
decided to swim into our blue.

My first born, dry fall girl
tumbled late into the season,
took charge on her own terms

Gathered waters from all
directions and channeled
a cleansing wash

My hips, now stiff, staunch
let waters slide over
what I know will be

The next phase of stone
letting go like the dry sand
lets go of other sand

With a soft push,
what I remember
of river, then and now

Is what stays beyond
is what rushes me in
is what cries me no river

Like no other river
like all rivers
like this river

Borne to bear
even me.

What I meant to say was

a jagged tooth from a craggy cliff
hooks a lip of cloud and
nature lovers taste each other

while down below
two abstract earthly
lovers gather
on the bridge

catching each
other on film, their
teeth bared with the rocks

Folk Tale

Black pond before dawn
Mirror in reverse

By diving into the
Heart of wet night

I could find myself
In the shock of wet glass

In water, licorice jello
Wobbly in a watery glaze

I expect to find an object
Stone unturned

Strand of hair from
Drowned maiden

Fishhook in a foot
Shard of ice glass

Discarded fin
Clichéd shoe

Nibbling lips of trout
To define and find me

Elated, smooth sand, only
Then, I dig in my toes in.

So this is how it goes after all.
Nothingness. Somethingness.

River by the Glass

The rush of tomorrow
Waves us on

We cannot see
The sea to see

The surge and swirl
Of what will be

What curls around the granite bones
And whirls amid the shiny stones

Kaleidoscope tumblers duly turn
And fingers burn

Eyelash spokes that rim the view
Peer close to crystalline askew

Colored glass bits
Rainbow flakes

Shards of reality hide behind
Spectacles offer a wink or two

Emeralds glance off
A curling wave

Float on top of filmy seas
Glassy bits of seamy dream

The camera clicks, emits a flash
And it will save a digital dash

Of what was that thing called?
Before disintegrating in the fall

Meanwhile a tumbler rests on crevassed
Edge aslant a granite wizened slab

With sky behind a bluish wash
Stick pine trees sway as tall as grass

We see it all through film and gauze
Illusion gives the lens some pause

To wonder whether river ever was
And blink it in regardless as

An image saved in a virtual folder
Floating into seas of older

The Fish

My father taught me how to swim to life
He must have seen my sudden fetal crawl
My body slicing membranes like a knife
While gasping choking wriggling in the squall

How I kicked my legs and broke his world
Beginning struggle at an early stroke
And like a butterfly in flight unfurled
To wings of infant innocence he spoke

Push off the heart he warned when leaving home
And turn like silver lest you lose retreat
Keep moving under water and its foam
So journey take you back where all ends meet

The backstroke takes you far into the start
The breaststroke brings you back into your heart.

Autumn on Bell Creek

II

On the Fence

I will follow the good side as far as the fire, but exclusively, if I can.

—Michel de Montaigne

On the Fence

On my walk I discover
a washed-out carcass of fox
in manzanita, willow,
scrub oak and toyon,
a mass of mingled fur and skin
with riotous bones in a gesture
of contempt, trapped there
in fine undergrowth of brush

There is a design in this path and
I wonder how it goes
think back to the long drives of adolescence
a world of wild moving outside the car window
at breakneck speed

All things animal on human terms:
granite outcroppings form
stone villages for ground squirrels
cedar fence posts make ramparts
for Red-winged Blackbirds
barbed wire embroiders scenery
with artistic surgery

One object unifies the landscape each time we pass
week after week, season after season
a sole fox hangs doubled on a top strand of wire
folded over like a coat on a bedstead,
waiting to be worn

I reflect on all the foxes of my life:
The Reynard, Tybalt, Aesop,
Disney, English hunting,
and even the Hughes, with its stink,
make this folded fox a real story

I thought, in my youthful outlook
that the fox just had bad luck
wasn't any good at being a fox
was perhaps a bad fox

Made a foxy mistake
misjudged the leaping space
wasn't foxy enough

Committed fox suicide in early foxhood
became a weasel in disguise
was outfoxed by other foxes
outfoxed himself

I begged my mother to stop the car
to get a closer look
because I had to see it

The triangular face,
slack jaw an opened wallet,
lips drawn into a sly smile,
eyes like my best shooter marbles,
fluffy tail for a perfect hat
paws dangling embarrassed,
tiny slivered claws

For years, I imagined the struggle
that moment of impaling
when the fox realized he was caught
and fox-life was all over

First, anger as the sting of the barbs cut into flesh,
then, excruciating pain before the blood thickened,
finally, calm resignation
as it mocked fate and
settled into death

I thought this myth into my adulthood
and that folded fox pressed on me for years
It was a guide,
a signpost for despair,
a warning of rough roads,
poor company,
leaps of faith.

And then, I lost my innocence hung on a line
in a conversation with a rancher when
he leaned up against the fence and grinned:

Little lady, let me tell you 'bout that fox:
That fox was shot for a thief
hung like a criminal
draped for show
slung in warning.

                 * * *

So it must be with this numb
jumble of a fox who now
finds himself in a bad fix

See how he folds over and
how easily he reeks weakness
beyond smell
beyond saving.

With a remnant of paw
and a marble eye
lies one of them,
one of us.

Marimba Mountains

Mallet of the steppes,
Heel and toe boot
Strike a granite chord

Let's say B-flat on
A table in the trail
Of jutting plates

Gives way to grey keys
Layered for
Paths of sound

Level by level
They rise to crescendo
A scale of root to root

Join limbs of note
In phrasing of pylon
To bind the soil at rest

A stone breaks loose
And tumbles below
Throwing off moss

Lichening, the descent
To an avalanche
Of arpeggio.

What Is to Wilderness

for Jane Hirshfield

I whisper to a fellow poet that I made love
to nature inhaling wind as it caressed me,
rubbed against a luxurious bush
of blackberry scratched and suckled
connected to the berry and laughed
as juices stained my chin

I've pressed against my cat who formed
my third breast without kneading

The poet, too, confesses that he placed a wad
of spit in his dog's mouth to put her at ease

I reply in kind that I kissed my cow's nose
slimed with half-chewed hay, dripping
white honey, one straw still stuck
to her swollen lip

Witnessed her bovine pleasure
as I scratched behind Hereford humps,
fingers of lost horn, her head down
stretching her neck for more as she
closed benign eyes

Content as cowbirds that searched her face
for sustenance, plucking insects, satisfied
as we were both satisfied loving nature as it was.

The kindred poet smiles and we rethink
a question of triadic equation
and ratio of universe
posed in a room of nature poets—

"Just what is to wilderness
as sex is to eros
as poetry is to language?"

The answer—a question—
of man's self love and thrust of
tongue into wind becoming
a pollinating irritant

Or is the connection some other random
flagellant taking a rubbing of sky,
perhaps a spinning mosquito
wanting a chance tryst on our behalf

Dying to inject a
little wad of spit
into the mix?

Chester and the Bluebird

Chester, that day
when you pressed your late
spring nose to the rim of the
black barbecue vessel

I sensed you were aware
of a twist in fate,
slated to become steak
and a future repast at last

It was a Gary Larson moment
with my mini-pitchfork in hand,
ring of bovine around me
circling the campfire

Kine as curious as cats
you all whiskered close
to the edge of the kettle
ready to singe a lip or nose

You were the boldest with
neck outstretched, juicy lawn forgotten,
when curled smoke dove into
wide, wet pink nostrils

Next moment a man drives up,
severed heads lolling in a side
compartment of his truck,
and asks, "Where is he?"

I lead him to your gate
after tempting you sorely
with a last alfalfa supper
that you leave unfinished

Then the settling of knives descends
and in forty-five minutes you are
hooked, hanged, loaded, dangling
done and undone.

Your relatives in the pasture
sniff drying blood of your passing
and mourn, as water drops slip
in red trails below their eyes

Three weeks later in true form
your replacement arrives
swaddled in white packages
nestled in solid brown crates

I sort each section of harvest:
the roasts, rump and chuck,
stew meat, fresh liver,
ground round

Then, the steaks:
rib, sirloin tip,
porterhouse, t-bone,
chuck, flank

Add a bag of bones
for the dogs, the cloven parts
neatly tucked into the upright
freezer with room to spare

The second coming arrives months later
the first barbecue of summer
rolls out the black kettle
like a dry cauldron

Tears spill over and
sizzle on the grill
when I try to lay that
first reluctant slab down

As the fork descends
a nearby looming pine sends
out a deep blue sprite shadow
to dance on my outstretched hand

The feather-soft blue bird
balances on my wrist, surveys
the grate then slips me the eye
and I freeze in still life.

What do you know, when
a kiss of sky alights,
rights itself, and then is gone
just like that.

What kind of moment
is it when the sky
bends down to
check on one of its own?

Deer in the Road

In a hurry on a dirt and gravel road
that bumps me around as usual
I almost hit a doe
who stops, ears raised, and
point blank stares at me

I brake and stop dead
only a few feet away,
engine off, and silence
between doe and woman
—a cord

I call her by name—deer—
through the open window
addressing that verdant desire
to speak in tongues
and meld into lush overgrowth

She listens intently
ears flick
eyes darken
nostrils flare
then, unconcerned, resumes

Nibble of scrub oak shoots
for what must be
my benefit and to put me at ease
as if to say, "I forgive you
your trespasses."

I start the car and she nimbly
flashes her back side
blending into brush
without a backward glance at the place
where near-accident and nature join

Fragment

The apple tree

snaps

in half

a fingernail

of the earth

broken

while I stand by

helpless

hair blowing

in the wind

still attached

Animal, Vegetable

You are what you eat—dead meat.
Vultured beef. Murder most fowl
gnaws on the last gristle of bone,
incisors pierce a lamb of slaughter,
and molars chew the fat while you chat.
Marbled steak beckons with
congealed fat of cudded alfalfa.

Look at yourself in a cellophaned mirror.
You struggle with some
abstract thought, serrated knife poised.

Token broccoli trees grace your plate.
A pretty tossed salad, with its
dewy lettuce and innocent tomato deceives.
You think the avocado a nice touch.
Slice in a hard-boiled egg and the kill begins again.

Somewhere a cougar coughs in the distance.
You turn your head slightly,
then pick up your fork, tuned.
You should never
ever leave your flesh
alone like that.

Four Levels of Mist

First level:

Above Squaw Valley
the ski slope and snowy retreat
once a real mountain
now a mere mountain semblance
in a brown gown
resorts to this:

Scouts for the new order
and a narrow view,
cumulus clouds dissipate
between two singular pines

Second level:

A bulldozer belches
blackening smoke
into shadow mist
that stayed beyond
its time

Third level:

A rusted pickup truck
in a particular hurry
its cloud of dust
an illusion
dissolves in
a casual wind
that just puts its lips together
and blows

Fourth level:

What will stay is on this level
as an empty black trash bag rolls
its own slick mass
across the cement path
and sucks up a breeze
that propels darkness

This heroic bag
will eventually flatten,
pass into guts and gas of earth
embedded as a permanent bubble
of mythological exhale

And this fourth level will be a
lasting mist in any valley.

Auto Archeology

Your steel—no, plastic—
Carriage will someday
Be found in a mound
Under soil

Evidence of who
You once were and
From what era

What will last?
Your plastic dashboard,
A thousand years

The interior of your
Glove compartment,
One year, max

With its kid gloves, maps,
CD case, gel pen,
Registration, emergency kit,
Bandaids, antenna fork,
Tissue packet,
Speeding ticket
Handicapped parking sign
Lipstick case
Tire gauge
Solar sunglasses

The steering wheel?
Give it a thousand years
Of spinning you full speed ahead
Into nothingness

Trees whirl by
Hurling you into a
Fast future if you're lucky—
Just where are you going, really?

Slow down and look around
People say as they peer through
And beyond you
To the next conversation

Keep your eyes on the road
And keep them peeled
Go with the flow they say

Hurl on modern man while you can
Before peripheral vision disappears and
Temple eyes dance a new form since it's
Too late for drivers.

Mouse Leaves

Mouse leaves
Run behind the
Tail of the truck
And scatter before winter
Commits suicide

The leaves die to live
In my mind

Rolling a yellow cat
Beneath my wheels
I feel my own bones crunch
And sink back into neck rest

The highway giveth quietly
And the highway taketh noisily

For the girl beneath the truck
May have mewed
Before she left
Before the yellow tarp
Announced her death

I think of my children and
Worry ahead for horrible
Fates down the road

But it is dark, the
Highway black
Rolling with only
Myself tonight.

Nails

Nails of my ancestors
raked the soil for grubs
  I clip them primly now
  so that I do not scratch
  my children

Nails of my ancestors
clawed bark from trees
  I file them so that
  needle points do not offend
  those afraid of witches

Nails of my ancestors
curved down to root
  Mine shoot out
  conical portraits
  for display

Ancient magic spirit-things
I throw you away in disregard
  Unwanted plant cuttings
  your loss does not worry me
  my ancestors swoon

They wring their hands
I am doomed, they moan

I buff my nails until they
shine in the night
        The wide-eyed faces
        of my ancestors
        crowd around

My ancestors cry
when I paint my nails red
        They pull out their skin and
        hold their heads in anguish

She has locked in her spirit
and is choking it in blood
        It comes off
        quite nicely, my dears

Poison! they gasp
        Remover, say I

They hold their noses against the toxin
with awkward paws, and fly away in haste
        I'm ready for some physical work, now
        typing is rough on the nails
        Oh, broke another one.

Bull Pine in the Window

Nothing dangerous will occur here inside
the kitchen, listening tightly for sudden snaps
in a passive pastoral

An open crown of a looming grey pine frames
wild cucumber and clumps of mule ear
that could pass for daisies
split trunks brush blue-iced sky
like a loose broom on a winter window
clearing morning crystal

Fingers borne in clusters of three
orchestrate wind with needle precision
and string the same sighs as an entire
stand of ponderosa, or a shadowy ravine
in an updraft of late afternoon

The Miwok call it ghost pine
non-Miwok call it the digger
defining backs of bent people
who gleaned its base and found
just enough sustenance

This bull pine is generous in its offering—
resiny spiked cones shaped like pineapple
to roast, scales open for sustaining seed
sweet kernels like prizes nestled in pairs
at the base of each husky segment
first-year cones seal spicy inner cores
as sap droplets ooze and harden into rock candy

This landscape leans into worry as
my need is the collection of parts—
bark, needle, cone—while ever darker
a shadow hangs above me in balance,
one hovering split-trunk limb haunts
every bone in my basket

The window, for now, will hold.

Solitude

Pick out one face
In the crowd of Sweet Williams
Like all the others
And it calls to you

What makes you choose
This particular one
For a brief moment
Of anomaly?

A slightly deeper purple
A more defined burst of white
A larger crown or taller stem
Sends its head higher than others

Maybe this one selects
You in the crowd of human faces
Choosing your face
From all the others

Sound Barrier

Jet spreads roar above
Starlings crackle

Distant car grumbles on a highway
Woodpeckers hammer

ATV grinds on a gravel road
Dove lifts one soft wing

Long whispers beyond us
Drone something deeper

Unknown
Beyond silence

Fall on North Fork, Tuolumne River

III

Mirror

I can feel my eye breaking.

—Robert Creeley

Mirror

       Hides its blackness
       Puts its glistening side
       Forward

As we do.

       Your face is
       In my eye
       And you see it, too.

So are you looking

       At me
       Or you?

Slow-pitch Poetry

You make contact with the word
with your tongue and
throw it to first base

In the field,
you catch the high fly, feel
it clump into your glove and form
another circle of speech complete

At bat there's a crack
and it's a fast grounder

Short stop receives the call
the gift of finishing the utterance
in one breath
the grounder going into
the stitched mitt
though you fear the bad hop of
a malaligned metaphor

There's the snap to first base
and the poet receives the throw—
It's an out, it's an out!

Softball wisdom
rushes to your head—
for the throw or pitch
catch or hit
words will flow

Softball wisdom feels
the sweet spot in the
mitt and at the bat

And knows you have
to wait for the word
to descend

Keep your eye
on it every second
and wait for it
to drop—

Wait for it,

until

you can hardly

stand it

Life of Letters

So complex this communication
Of six e-mail addresses
Cell phone voice mail
Portable phone, message service

Mailbox paper mail, snail mail
Wooden cubicle of office mail
An answering machine,
Twitter, Flitter, Flicker, Ning, Bing
Bang, Google, Froogal, Facebook,
Racebook, Myspace, Yourface,
Yourplace or Myplace

My neighbor waves without
Seeing me—wait, too late
My eyes intent on potholes
And missing her fender in
A narrow squeeze of road

The dogs greet me tails away
Bodies shake in pleasure
Their heads tilt up to
Receive greeting palms

And their tongues
Taste my wanderings
And exchange theirs
My head between two wet
Noses sniffing home

The cat sniffs my stockinged
Feet and washes a greeting
Her tongue sticking
In nylon mesh

My husband kisses
Me his hello and smiles
Twinkle eyes full
Of news of the day
Spilling over
Into the best
Message ever.

Eye Think

        The eye must think
        before it can see,
        says the artist.

I see what you mean, artist,
but I fail to see the significance
of what you are
thinking.
My eye has no brain

        You would be surprised
        says the artist
        winking thoughtfully

My eye is a window.
Windows don't think

        The artist blinks
        then closes his eyes
        for a moment

What are you thinking?

        His eyes fly open

        I am thinking about
        my next art work

        The artist looks at
        a blank white wall

   Oh, I see.
   I see that, too,
    illusion is everything

Now, you've lost me.
Look, if eyes had brains
they'd walk.
They certainly wouldn't
hang around here

    Brains don't have legs, he muses.
    The artist looks at his blank work
    while deep in thought

I picture his painting walking
off the white wall in my view.
By the way, I say
Isn't that blue a little dark?

    Close your eyes, says the artist
    Now tell me what you think

My brain blinks, once.
Twice.
It is still dark.

    The artist squints,
    shakes his head.
    His brains walk back
    onto the wall.
    The window closes.

Drop of Moon

Three young poets
want to be immortalized
in a poem of their own

Dropped into place
in an amber drop of time
where moon guides
linings of minds

Alexia bears the blue earth
in her eyes weighing place
with purpose and lingering there

Tiffany blends exotic longing
into prose containing her soul

Nichole, the shadow one
with night pools for eyes
closes the dark inside

All three carry essential light
willing to ignite right there
suspended in an amber drop
of moon waiting for some sign

To move into the world
the way they want to
move into it so it stays

This drop, this poem
one collected period
of their awareness stays
and keeps them in one space

Even when they move
into the next phase
inevitably new

A Poet

A poet begins to eat herself
In the carton of amuse
She opens the container
And having but a spoon, begins
To dip into drying flakes of moon
Scrutinizing each scoop
Before the bite and the chew

Know thyself, she sputters

A poet knows the workings of
The cosmos but cannot
Find her shoes
She cannot find the rhythm
Of the man-made day
As it walks her

Out of sync
Out of step

A poet is a package
In mismatched wrap
She vibrates in her box of bones
Picking at the prize

She is not the cereal
You think she is
Inside

A poet does not completely
Eat herself
And for that
No one is unnerved
At breakfast

Alignment

Is not like having your wheels aligned
Or your back cracked into place again.
Is not like teeth, white pillars that
Lean and overlap in our youth
Linked by civilized metal that frames
An acceptable straight smile.

Alignment is not your father coming up
Behind you and pushing that knocked knee
Loose again
Giving to the world another slant
Avoiding unladylike bowed legs
So unattractive later.

Your mother's words reverberate:
Stand up straight
Walk with your feet facing
Forward, not out like a duck
Not pigeon-toed like your friend
Who pulls into herself with shy restraint

Alignment is not marching lockstep to beliefs
Of a group or the clicking together
Of heels from the past, to some possible
Genetic warlike penchant of warrior memory

It is your own new map
Your personal skeletal makeup
A frame for generations to come
That glues your parts into what
Looks to be you.

What sharp bones move us to collection?
I sometimes hear femurs clacking
In protest, when I think I know what
They want but ignore them.
They are loud.
They rattle into the future.

They are fused together with
The glue of pure pluck.
Slipping off
Somewhere else
Putting one foot in front of the other
Walking in uncomfortable shoes
That wear weary from gravel roads

Alignment comes after ordering your calves
To go one more mile without burning
Or else you will just stop in the middle
Of the path and simply curl up into a fetal
Ball and refuse to move at all

Veer up and go straight and narrow
On that balance beam, on the fine trapeze line
Straight into eternity with an arrow of light
Dancing the crooked horizon

Glass

Half full half empty
Half of what it could be should be
Did be empty be
Glassy once in your life
Half of your life
Not in a half life
Empty be
Take that glass and empty it
Once it is empty
Fill it till it is empty
Water down the full crystal, baby

Transcendental Perch

I pose a profound question
to the high school class of junior thinkers,
but five are asleep, dreaming into desks
arms bent below their heads making nests
while I read lulling passages from Walden
the parts where the ants do battle on a chip,
where the loon croons its lonely song in partnership
with the man who studies sudden appearances
in the water and reflects on these things

The Myrmidon battle between the red fire ants
and the lone black warrior ant
rages on and while combatants are fully engaged
snoozing militants suddenly awake from resting places
in crooks of arms, but when there is no clear winner
of the wood chip, interest wanes

Life returns with a promise of violence
I tell them to be patient, brutality is coming as
a giant hand lifts us onto a windowsill

During the snap of the black ant leg
desk warriors call out from the perimeter
He's down, he's hurt, he won't make it!
They laugh at loss of antennae as
Trojanic spectators jeer and Helens sigh
and review their painted nails
while a watching Greek pouts—not his game

In the meantime, air-conditioned wind waves us on and
I speak in earnest, resonating with great heft and breath
that *this is the world* here on the windowsill
as my voice lifts to heroic heights

I paint a picture of a pre-twilight Thoreau
scene of my own in the woods of my dreams

Imagine this, I tell them—
A Western Kingbird is frozen on a pine bough
and basks in an afterwash of sun as he
grips the branch tightly
and keeps his beak to the West

(I pause for effect)

So, my young philosophers, I tell them—
I wonder if it is altogether possible
that wild birds perchance happen to meditate?

(There is quiet in the room)

I rephrase this profound question thinking
they have not really listened and ask again
in simple words meant to stir their hearts and minds,
in separation of search and state

Do birds acknowledge their god with a nod?

(Vacant silence)

I persist, heading into dangerous air for public schools—
At great peril for the sake of my career

Does a woodpecker reflect on his maker?

(And finally a stirring and whirring
of words at last from the mass)

A student drones in a low monotone
You said it was a Kingbird.
Something inside of me dies there

The fledglings at their desks shift positions
deep thought permeates—so thick
so quiet that in my momentary wisdom
I decide to move the air one more time

I clear my throat simply and in desperation
with conviction in my voice, I reverberate
take a risk of falling from my place of comfort

Does that bird have a god?

I can hear the rafters shake and
all manner of yellow birds swoop down
in remembrance of an earlier crucible study

One enlightened Cambodian student
suddenly lifts his head off the desk,
his eyes appear brightened by a thought

I anticipate ancient Asian wisdom
and grip the podium in excitement
as the sense of a pending reflective
answer electrifies my very being

As the summer afternoon sun streams onto his face
that certain Dickinson slant of light hits him
the boy disentangles angelic selfhood from desk wood
and his own thin arms, and awakens and speaks

God? Yes—he's got a god.

(The whole room listens, rapt and bound)

I press silently, first, then open the cage

Yes, good, all right, and what is that god?

He pauses, looks around at his fellow followers,
Licks his lips, and opens his mouth

You know—he smiles a certain wisdom—
a bigger bird.

I laugh so hard I fall off my perch as
the whole class is laughing
because I'm laughing
in order to fathom the wisdom
in all manner of birds
laughing in that room.

Eye

A doughnut does not know
That it exists

It does not know that it
Contains a cosmic eye

A wink encircles the hole
A moment
Then it is not a wink

Eyelashes
Bicycle spokes

On the outside
Of two dark planets

In milk space
Narrowing, wid en ing

If you eat the doughnut
And the hole as one
As you must
The hole hovers,
But where?

The hole becomes the something
Around which nothing
Could fasten itself

Nose in the center of the flower
Thrown stone in the pond

Pencil point to mirror
Wooden spoon in the soup pot

With a name it
Could lose itself

Suddenly it becomes the core
Of the blue flower on the
Tablecloth

The cooked yolk rolls out
Of the sliced egg like a wheel

It comes to rest in the center of
The flower on the tablecloth

It is the cosmic guffaw
The round bellowing

Of a rolling eye wrapped
In a flour of invisibility

It is the eye of my forehead

Love and Finance

—an investment venture

Options open into trust
A wink, a thrust
In someone's direction
Shapes capital

She wanted security
In principle
But ventured too far
Into interest

What were the options:
Futures exchanged for profitability
A margin of error maybe

What would redeem her value
What would insure her safe deposit,
And accrued investment

Her assets spill like liquid at a rate
Growing in interest but lacking in trust
Mutual ambition will fund his eyes

Stocks split into late profit
Yields rebound briefly
Performance is flexible
Equity bonds too much

He looks elsewhere
A trade for gains
Her loss at issue
Evaporates into

No guaranty
No disclosure
No dividend
No fidelity

The account matures
In the balance
Withdrawal is complete.
Account closed.

Beauty and the Beast: The Movie

A movie Panzer tank pauses while
just over the crest the enemy rolls into view

The Sousa piece whistles and
pipes up the Stars and Stripes Forever

A blur of dust drifts as tanks roll in
while a filmic vision forms:

Perched on the enemy tank gun
posed luxuriously on the American barrel

A voluptuous girl waves a scarf at the men
her graceful legs angled into a wishbone

She beams into the glare of sun
and shades her eyes with a hand

Teutonic warriors beyond the hill
squint into raw light and behold her as

The girl arches back her head and laughs
and a strip of hair catches across her lips

Like a strap loose in the wind
trying to attach itself once again

At this moment the Panzer tank gunner
watches her as she comes over the rise

Floats into his own picture
and he blinks hard and swallows

This girl could be his lover, sister
daughter, mother—this girl, his girl

Becomes every girl and he waits
for command—for direction from above

Lili Marlene sounds in the background
and every soldier knows that song

A drop of wet salt slides down in one trickle
and burns his eye as he squints at the target

Teeth clench and he captures a breath as
one small muscle on his jaw twitches

The moment drones as he waits
for orders and he wavers

Just enough
but not enough

To save her from the horror of order
before he blows her to oblivion

Remnants of

lace
        satin
                garter

drift down

        at
                random

With that last dramatic clip
the director lights a smoke

His fingers shake in their own war
as they flicker black and white

He bites his lip and swallows a slip
of his own skin and thinks

Of his own women in their frames
and thinks that for this film

This particular girl, maybe,
should be French

Clavey Waterfall

IV

From the Other Side

*When breath blew back,
And on the other side
I heard recede the disappointed tide!*

—Emily Dickinson

From the Other Side

I'm calling from the jail cell
I want you to know I hate you all

Dishes in boxes, the mirror packed
Books in crates, wait to be cracked

I won't be staying in this place where I'm at
I want to go home and see my cat

Christmas ornaments wrapped in tissue paper
Dusty letters unearthed much later

I hate the daughter who put me here today
I'll get a lawyer and take her house away

The opera records scattered and lost
The TV console rescued, almost tossed

They'll see what will happen when I get done
I'll fire the quack who won't let me go home

Sturdy shoes and pastel pantsuits boxed
Photo albums packaged, items crossed off

Do I have my home anymore and my rings?
What have they done with all of my things?

Overstuffed sofa goes to goodwill racks
Cat-hair recliner makes the dumpster stacks

I want to go home.
Will you help me go home?

Loved ones haggle the paintings and end tables,
China, silver, plates all have labels

Do I still have a home?
Where is my phone?

Throw out the dusters, cat box and more
Pillows and braid rugs, junk by the store

I want to go home.
Help me go home.

Cat's at the pound, not at the neighbors
No one comes forward to return all the favors

I'm getting out of here soon as I'm better
My lawyer's going to be getting my letter

The realtor visits, inspects the rugs
Looks like we'll have to be spraying for bugs

The food here is fine, but they can't cook worth beans
I'm getting out tomorrow, you wait and see

Medicare takes care of most of the bill
What isn't covered, the kids maybe will

I'm feeling just fine, now where is my cat
I'm not going to stay here wherever I'm at

She'll live on for years says the medical team
Her heart is in great shape and so is her spleen

Where is my home? I'm chilled to the bone.
Where is my cat? I can't be alone.

Black Dog

The black dog arrives three times
in succession:

I.

I hurtle down the highway
then the dog noses into my car
and disappears after a thud

The bruised car grazes by the roadside
still ticking and steaming
while highway asphalt shimmers

II.

Next time weeks later he lopes up our dirt road
gives a backward glance, tongue lolling red
his legs a machine

He clearly vanishes after
headlight beam and eye shine
expose him as shadow

III.

Take this holy water, my friend insists
it will protect you from the black dog
her hand shakes with the weight

And passes over a plastic Wishbone
bottle with a Jesus cut-out
pasted to the label

IV.

I sprinkle her blessed water over thresholds
lines of entry and all windows
doors and openings, save some

But the dog comes for my friend's son
and too late I wonder about shelf life,
code dates for holy water, and if it is still good

Fire Safe

Friends of the victim say
It was a tragedy
He died a hero

Engulfed in flames he was
Crackling with wood sparks
While the whole sky lit up

A woman screamed in second story
Then cried much later over
Damaged remains

He extracted her to safety all right
Threw her out the window hard
Dumped her while he could

They had their domestic squabbles
Romanticized stones into façade
Stories spun out of control

The frame collapsed finally
Ashes drifted to a home
Somewhere else.

Returning from Iraq

A nineteen-year-old warrior
Fresh out of high school
Kills and lives and
Takes home medals
To put on his shelf
With his Legos
And Transformers

He is home for the holidays
But will go back to Iraq
And he asks the class
Of innocents
What they think of
Privatization of armies.

Need Fire

—for Michael Dedini

He set the clock ticking too soon and too late
The minute was off in a skipped beat of fate

With a column of ivory dominoes tipped
He knew the dark numbers and knew that he'd slip

But he wanted to make that configuration anyway
Branching out chances for luck every day

As his lungs and limbs struggled
And his trunk and heart splintered

He loved too much, that he did, all his life
He suffered too much, and so did his wife

And he could have complained that God was unfair
Measuring sand in his glass of thin air

But he didn't and drank the dust God had given
Thirsty and thankful, love had him driven

To shape the family of clay clustered around him
To offer his friends a full cup to the brim

To remind us at last, of the mission we're gifted
To live in the memories of hearts that we've lifted

That we're electric stardust enclosed in a frame
Heavenly fire to dry out the rain

He suddenly shook off the yoke of affliction
Softened his voice, whispered hopeful conviction

From darkness to light, he lit the need fire
From ignorance to knowledge, he climbed to the pyre

He danced the St. Vitus' dance, leapt the flame
To shield us all from the darkness and pain

His circle of sunlight spun life in its swath
His bright wheel ignited gilt hills in its path

The need fire sparked out eternal protection
And after its embers died down, resurrection

Let's light all the torches in his own good name
And toast to his essence, forever a flame.

Haiku-Like

I.

The brown hills
Of the Mother Lode
Are tight-fisted hands
With hidden rings

II.

The red moon
Caught in a cloud
Like a wound in a bandage
My heart frees itself

III.

The smell of sunburned grass
In the evening
My nostrils make tornadoes
Sweeping across the field

IV.

Pay Per View

The television in the creek
Presents an ecological episode
A squirrel watches himself
In the glass, preening
In mere black and white

V.

Black Cloud

Fifty vultures gather together
To migrate this morning
Must be lack of sustenance
Here at the River of Skulls

Battered Woman

Butterfly blue
your wings of wall shadow
sun-tipped edges glow
illuminating your outline of life
essence remains
on the outside

The slow moan of
your opening
wings spread
from the pain of touching

Butterfly violet
you've hit the wall
joined your shadow
in bruise paint
of velvet down

Repose of collect
the pin put in perspective
revealing a narrowing slit
pulsing purple
and red
alternately, quietly

Butterfly yellow
jagged spirit alight
glancing below
at a dark past
Pasted to the pillowed wall
flowers mingling, dancing
waving you back

Ragged, separated,
severed,
cut free by a decision
to leave
the comfort of suffer
the pin retaining
your flesh,
your wings become your life.

A trail of red
jet stream outlining your pattern
of departure
fading stain
becoming the sunset
and the crimson sunrise
signaling a storm of renewal

Is this an Icaral dream of flight
or are the walls moving down
and around like stacks of stones
defining your imprint
Butterfly blue?

Food for Thought

How many tablets would it take?
She tumbles ten in her grown hand
They shine in the light, pink and white
This is no way to prescribe sorrow

At ten she brings in the tray
For an infected mother, offers
Ice water with lemon, a muffin
Topped with a comfortable pat of butter

The poached egg timed perfectly
As she had been dutifully taught
A handful of just-picked begonia blossoms
With too-small stems slipping in the wet glass

Later in life she would slip off her dress
Discard the handful of false hope instead
And peel into the waiting world blind
Naked pushing through 1 AM darkness

Leper Lady at Swiss Park

The drunken rotund man dances with the leper lady
her nose nearly gone, ears like chewed leaves
pieces gone from edges of dissolving skin
as if worms sheared them away while she spun

She is thin and swirls with her lips,
holding onto her skin in the spin.
His excess envelops her as they both
take up space on the floor

She is dainty dry in a rustling dress.
He simmers in his own juices.
The two together like that
dancing as one disappears
and another gains substance

I dance with the scrawny boy
who whispers, "Dare you to touch her."
So I bundle up in horror and weave myself
up close to touch her skirt, and it doesn't crumble

"No, her skin," he hisses.
We dance near and I brush her bare leg
softer than a baby after a bath
growing new

When I meet her startled eyes
my own skin turns brittle.

Navajo Traveler

There was a plan from the stars down
Then came the sun and moon
According to Navajo ways
And my friend sought them both

Taking dark paths of bramble, then stone
Next the clay, and the smooth one
Giving harmony in song rumbling down
In the earth from a much larger yawn

To the Navajo, early man wanted a strong life
From the perfect turquoise emerged the sun
One piece of white shell became the moon
A fingernail that guided her on starless nights

My Navajo friend carried the US mail
And messages to people held in her bag
The white sealed envelopes of buried story
From box to box she delivered daily

She carried the news,
The trappings of lives
Shall I send you smoke signals, she wisecracked
And laughed, her teeth dazzled as white as the mail.

Now she carries the news from beyond
Reminds us to cherish
Every moment we are here
For it is brief, an unopened envelope

She carries the news to her father long gone,
Who visited her often in living night dreams
As tribe princess tells stories to her people at rest
The blood of her daughter will carry beyond her

We try to climb mountains to get closer to heaven
But she climbed the four mountains of her ancestors' lines
The four mountains of four directions in its four seasons
And each mountain its song she sang in good time

My friend doubled up in secrets of her past, of her family,
Of her sorrows, and gave pieces to us all, like jewelry borrowed
Of silver, or turquoise, like stones, like rough splintered bone
And shell rings and necklaces with essence of life

She gave away all of the pieces of herself
Silver ringlets for wrists and enveloping bands
Lizards sunning on rocks with circling tails
Sheared wool from the sheep, to weave into blankets

Shards of bright pottery winking in sand
Puffs of dry cloud, caught on yucca blossoms
Pieces of fry bread folded in hand
Songs of volcanic lava, laughter chipping off

She told her old stories, protected her secrets
Shared our old news and back to her ancestors
Like news from the busy red earth, the ants speaking
In flurries, in a hurry to get to their leaving

Stories for her father
Stories for healing
Stories for truth
Stories for mistakes made

Stories for landscape,
Stories for partaking
Stories to envision the possibility
Of impossible things

Stories she gives lives on in our dreams
In her youth, her bountiful days with the sheep
In old herding times that taught her to know
The value in shearing, of taking life to give life

Now she floats in the soft fleece of lamb
Perfectly happy—floating wool of the new blanket
Floating like the feather from a dropped wing—
Maybe a blue jay

There is strength in solitude and she whispers this advice:
Do not be afraid to be alone—as we are
Maybe she will come to us
Some nights in our dreams

Or in our day thoughts
Like streams over silver boulders
To tell us stories of her new place
Her new face. Maybe not.

She is with the wind now
And sings back the song that blows love
But not leaving, telling us
It is perfectly fine to let go.

Piercing

Rings wrap round to trap good spirits
Reject the old ghosts
Connect pieces of flesh
And weave silver posts to their place

A stud through the tongue
Curbs a mouth's pure speech
While mumbling ball of gold rolls
Dull words that tumble home

In this way the body sieve
Leaks spirit, oozes its soul
One more hole in the nose
Will drown one yet

The palms face up next
Then go for the crown
Feet face the fencing
Limbs wrapped in chain

Barbed wire links to fettered life
Pens her into her own godly flesh
Yet she is a paddock without any flock
And waits for the next metal lock

It doesn't hurt, she smiles,
Her teeth once held braces
Her friends in the needled arts
Bare all their flesh wounds

The black holes of orifices,
Armed punctured saviors
Without a doubt leak something
Seek new birth places.

Emergency procedures
For deep puncture wounds:
Apply direct pressure
To help stop the flow

Dare we say that love of the needle
Makes the stakes sharper, and ever deeper,
Hurries the journey to the next dark place
Where one more prick takes her down forever

Tuolumne Meadows Bridge

—En Route to Parsons Memorial Lodge

Julie is the first to call out manhood while
The nearby peak flexes its muscles

We imagine a nipple ring on one of the
Perky twin peaks—Gaea's breast with
Sucking infant gods attached like clouds

How she must have worked to produce
The vista for our viewing pleasure
Wheezing in wind, the sky pressing
Her to bear even more blue

Salt and pepper granite
Molds my new shape into
Stones to stay the river

An anniversary couple
Locates the exact spot
They married in the meadow
Last year and Gaea
Nods approval through
Eyelash pines as witness

Julie suggests we add scrotum
In all fairness, to the poem

Reclining, the river glitters
As if to say,
Move me
Why don't you.

Gods Bath, Clavey River

V

The Long Dance

Call it, once more, a river, an unnamed flowing,
Space-filled, reflecting the seasons, the folk-lore
Of each of the senses; call it, again and again,
The river that flows nowhere, like the sea.

—Wallace Stevens

The Long Dance

—for Otto and Magdalena

Ja cię kocham, a ty śpisz
I love you, but you are sleeping
The woman said to the man in the shadows
In another language she thought
He did not understand

But he did understand
And waited for her
Dreamy-eyed

Later days, on a train, they met again
He eyed her two Bock beers
Longingly—she noticed his glances
And gave him a bottle

They have been drinking in love
That way since that second meeting
Giving so much more than they
Thought they would have left to give

That first date, watching *The Third Man*
In a dark theatre, hands clasped
They risked belonging to a dream
Of love that would stay the years

Leaving the mother country
Visions of new life
Sent them packing
Weaving struggle and sacrifice
Into shifting patterns of fabric

In looking back
Along the wake of track
Stormy seas rocked their craft
Spinning out a rough course

What kept them so young
Was it hands, never still?

Was it the praying hands he carved her
In wood, or the fixing of all things
That stopped working

Was it the cooking and scrubbing hands
That created magic fruit cobblers in the kitchen
To satisfy a sweet tooth in the morning?

Was it the joy of life they preserved like
Jellies in the cellar and fermenting
Elderberry wine by the gallon?

Smooth waters now flow
In a soft golden glow
Of shimmery road
Between homes of love

They laugh and toast
Crystal glasses cling-cling
As family and friends cluster close

Together, the two lovers dance
Through fifty golden years
And waltz down days
That glisten just for them

Song for Sisters

1.

In my shadow, I thought you were a dancing
extension of myself
a delicate, dark, quiet mass that moved
with me, but now I think we are merely
placeholders between two worlds
taking turns fading in the light

We came from the fire, remember?
little Teutonic fireballs
wanting to spit, learning to sputter

Not being in your wedding photo was a sign
of my helplessness,
in not unraveling the rope,
your time charred

2.

The dog ruled your childhood day with impetigo
and his teeth made a track of stitches after your
warm blood stained the snow of Christmas
his toenails clicked across the cement slab
and followed you not out of love
but out of a need to scratch

Remember when we sang the cruel sister song
when she drowned her fair double in the river?
Who could fathom such a horror?
Not a one-eye, two-eye, three-eyes song
not the cruel stepsisters of the pumpkin coach song
not the light and dark sisters song

This is the song of the fair and lovely sisters
the brash and billowy sisters
the plush and lean sisters
who would dissolve the dog in fire
with just his teeth for stars.

There is a Cough

There is a cough in the back bedroom
My child cries out
Part of me gets up and goes to her

But most of me is actually still
Here by the window
With the sun on my shoulder

The wind is cold out there
It blew in my face this morning
When I opened the door.

Crying won't help her cough
Why is she crying then?

I am still in the chair
In the sun
And it feels good.

I should go back
And nurture her.

But the sun is primevally warm
And I'm a grey lizard on an
Orange stone turning orange.

Sometimes the clock ticks
And sometimes a car roars.
Only sometimes.

I reach for the curtain
Push it aside greedily for more sun
The clock stops ticking

Now it is ticking again
Because I hear it

I also hear a child coughing
It is my child
My child is coughing.

What Yeats Knew

You are both extremely fertile
an astrologer once whispered
awestruck by lines of suns and moons

You could create at least ten new beings
the numerologist gushed, just
look at the weight of the water signs

I saw plains and valleys
waving amber wheat and grain
rushing rivers and pools
forming from the rain
and everywhere signs

Fill up with water here, signs
flood signs, no fishing signs
bridge signs and river signs
swift current signs
no swimming signs
all manner of water signs

When the first one arrived
she was slow in seeing the signs
the second one waited for another signal
the third leaped into life before the signing
and arrived like a sailing salmon upstream

The signs will line up soon and post for the leaving
and suddenly, I'm not in too much of a hurry
to read them at length by the light of the moon
or pore through my horoscope relaying news
or play by the numbers that hint of sure doom

Father

Prenatal

He watched from the outside
As I swam inside
The breast stroke
The crawl
He watched
As I swam out
Wriggled
Gasped
Choked

Parental

This is the crawl he spoke
The fastest stroke
Kick your legs
Pull your arms
Cup your hands

This is the breaststroke
Push out from the heart

This is the butterfly
Unfold your wings

This is the backstroke
Retreat sometimes

Paternal

My father the fish
Taught me how to
Stroke ripples
Blow bubbles
Gulp quickly
Push away
And swim back

The Ritual of Coffee Making

A light in place of the sun
Opens doors on cubic floors
A trickling of water announces the morning
Of coffee coming into our world
Your hands
Measure endless spoons
Of burnt sienna granules
The carafe waiting patiently
For the first burst of ah.

You pour the fall right into my cup
Cascading, filling the deep yawning cavern
Then our words burst

Slippered and robed
We rub each other's
Sleep from eyelashes
Laughing at how crusty we have become
Trusting that the machine
Will not break down
Not this morning

You vary vanilla and crème brûlée
Taste it, you say,
Is it okay?
My lips purse and sip at the mug
With a small taste of edge
To say, this will be
A brimming day.

Bull Pine

Just outside the bedroom window
a grey pine determines our space

As two limbs lean
poised over this frame
in a private painting

I think the sky will fall today
my love thinks the tree may
fall the other way

There is a curve at this horizon
doubt does not make love safe, I say
hope is a thing with needles, he says

As the wind comes, we wager
this way, that way

Even one limb could snap
pleasure in two I warn

He groans and turns
while wind subsides

A Living

The good German daughter leaves the loft
begging for potatoes or a cup of milk
for her baby and for her aging mother

A swollen grandmother in a rat-infested room
cradles the infant, waits for more bombing
waits patiently for the good daughter's return

One farmer says no
the next, again no
we don't have enough

Says his wife too evenly
but offers a potato
with too many eyes

The next door another
pitying stare gives a cup of milk
that will make for a day

The good daughter dodges blasts
and runs with meager treasures
slipping from numb fingers

She flies to the apartment
hoping it is still there
a cell with its honey intact

The baby coos and gurgles to
grandmother humming and
rocking as she stops and looks up

So this was existence then
with small pleasures to be had
from a potato with too many eyes

From little milk of human kindness
in a land where *Arbeit Macht Frei*
and American bombers have their orders.

Photo Album Leaves

Mother young there are stages
in which my body acts like you
twists its own way into something else
wind-blown hair, wise-acre once-eighteen smile

Darker shadows than the war can form
congeal beneath a charcoal coat
one gold tooth flashes black among ivory
keys to your historical percussion

My daughters step to your nightened rhythm
for one may someday hear a motor hum
in a dark garage

Or another may slip out the pills
and just before succumbing
break into a naked run
shedding old ways like first skin
peeling off well-meaning old world plaster

Maybe future daughters will reel in kind and
snap back the elastic wrap
of original package and
envelop a new order of
celluloid skin for their movies.

This is called future and we're all going there.
Daughters, hold your aprons and hang onto stairs

Mother old, and yours before,
I may have your nose,
the set of lips, the hips
the jowls and scowls
the deeper lines of your mouth
heading south

One daughter already has your proximity
to ground and the smell of soil
and oil in her hair
The other, a proclivity
toward steel-driven eyes that still
can iron over a wrinkled will

Genetics have probably gone awry
with elements snaking far into surprise
my limbs begin to follow in yours
and I am coming back to you as I speak
with a tooth shunning gold
a womb lined with mold

My daughters line up for the family photo,
await a magical transformation,
in a shadow world of their own making.

Still time for another photo
to line up grins and
make room for
the little ones down in front.

Moon Predictions

Truth dangles so low in the sky
It digs its fingernail into the slack
Fabric of the night
Catching right there

One tooth shines before
Biting into a black apple

A light in a nearby cottage window
Gleams over the rise

A spoon in the soup steals
Before the ladle lowers

One jettisoned cat claw
Surprised into carpet

You remember the tarot reader
The poem you wrote about her
But more about you

Lessons bode ill
As her dirt-laden nails
Turned each signifier card

Of sword
And prince
Showing one who would
Steal away your name

Like so many words
Her predictions turned to dust
And who was that prince
Riding into destiny
With thighs working
And load shifting?

Navajo Gifts

Our friendship, a trade
Of dinner and dinner
You give Zuni bread loaf, round and full
I give advice at midnight
You give a silver necklace of wild rose
And I, more words from the heart

"Do not lose this" sing your even white teeth
Silent piano keys harmonize
With woven brown fingers painting air
As beads circle in my pale palm

You sizzle fry bread
I boil Teutonic dumplings
Our glasses clink twice
During the reservation video
Your grandmother bedecked in turquoise
The sound of trickling water over stones
Speaking of relatives

Your round face, mistaken for Filipino
Mexican, Polynesian but actually Navajo
Denied service in lines of pale faces
You elbow for a place enveloping two worlds
Sweeping the path for your child of both minds
Woven from a duo of ancestral designs

Your people spoke cipher over mine long ago
But we don't converse in code when we laugh
And tell jokes about ourselves
Although it just occurred to me
I don't even know your Navajo name

Desert Bloom

—For Dorothy Rose

There she is, just as she ever was
Like surprise of a delicate bloom
Bending from a breeze in the room
And a familiar forward slant
Of going somewhere too soon

We see her still, as teapot steams
And crossword puzzle uncrosses itself
Toward a letter to a friend perched on the table
Next to a new novel, freshly unopened
While the cat pauses near his dish

She would probably tell us all
Not to waste precious time weeping
To save the water for the garden in divine heat
To save it for ourselves when days go dry
As things are perfectly fine so don't worry

There she is, just as ever she was
Kneels in the garden, pinches off dry blossoms
Hauls the water hoses to a better place
Removes choking weeds and thins the ever too lush
Fertilizes naturally and trims the wayward bush

She is still here, near, just as all molecules still are here
Like all cells and bells were ever here just as
When snowflakes spin into diamonds,
And sunlight sends news turning one more page
When electric stars ignite one more night

There she is, in memory, in still life
Inviting us to tea, still hot, and why not
The cups laid out, fine as you please
With the heavy work done and overly undone
Just drink with her now, and kindly take your ease.

Coming into Love

Glass after glass in succession
coming into love is a great
thrill of water
pouring
into
rows of glasses from a pitcher above

>From the spout of a sea jar
a kind of stream
in mid-air
and a splash
clean, spritzing

The water continues its fill
surrounds what is inside
a virtual ocean emptying its jar of suds
of clear excess froth

>You blow the foam from
your beer and it sprays out
in Neptune glory with
amber liquid visible
inside glass

Your lips lathered at the rim
you can see through me
through the invitational glass
eyes glittering
behind the mug

    The filling subsides
    as the pitcher rights itself above
    and glasses disappear

Some bubble is drizzling
down the side
your finger catches the rivulet
and you laugh since you cannot stop
the flow

Accidents of Moon

1.
When the muse chooses to arrive
it is not always convenient

>On Highway 99, sudden utterances search for more
>than the back of a greasy grocery receipt
>to record quickening pieces of mind
>tumbling and tumbling like
>lottery numbers for losers
>I nearly swerve out of my lane it's that good

Thoughts of importance loom
the day I swelled with pride
when my mother said I
could help her pick apples in
the supermarket bin and when
we plucked them out of the bag she sighed
so many bruised ones, flawed in some way
I knew no one would take them home.

2.
I tell my daughter that accident must be insight
when that double tractor-trailer semi-truck
smashed her too early into herself, compressed
her into her own double before she could even scream

I tell her she began that way, as a surprise
spilling plans, her love too great to wait for later

"Oh, Ma," she sighs and we
sit there, holding each other in time.

3.
I go about the business of day waiting
for the slap of little epiphanies to push life
back into me

>	In the new moon
>	the Hokusai print is not
>	illuminated on the dark
>	bedroom wall
>
>	an oval attempt
>	to see what is not
>	is some comfort

This blank space, a small gift, an O of moment
serves as cipher to hold the place
while I should be doing something useful
like filing grocery receipts in proper boxes
or peeling imperfect apples for pie,
accidents waiting for the next one.

Rapid Detail, Tuolumne River

VI

You *Can* Take It With You

But if something does flash before your eyes
As you go under, it will probably be a fish,

A quick blur of curved silver darting away,
Having nothing to do with your life or your death.

—Billy Collins

You *Can* Take It With You

Exhibit One: Repose

Imagine a favorite chair
your body curved into a seated form
an adoring cat
an open book flat
about to turn a page
a pool of light
spilling over the brim

This could be a sculpture
set on a shelf in a shadow box
a limited edition of ten
a gift for a friend
to remember in

Twelve thousand years
of dust and voila you're in a museum
on a shelf, with a tag and a label
"Ritual Sacrifices in America"

Maybe they think
you were a goddess
with your legs hooked in a bow
like that with the cat and the book,
your pedestal below

Exhibit Two: Commercial Break

Next to you looms another still life
a tableau of a ritual family
prone in front of a blue box
staring into tomorrow

They put you in juxtaposition there
next to the typical American family
and you cannot change the station

Exhibit 3: Love

Peruvian drinking vessels
made for corn beer
so many libations of maize
it would make your head spin

But no image of the female anywhere
except in one isolated vessel:
a rutting stag shades a curious doe
with a face not fully carved

Plaque after historic plaque proclaims
fertility as being vital to this society
and not a single female to be had—
it must be oversight

Exhibit 4: Hereafter

The mummified Egyptian priest
still has head hair, toenails, teeth
stretched skin thin with room to grow
black leather taut against his cheek

The ivory was worth saving
but bread had to be tough
with small stones
wearing away enamel
down to his nerve

The afterlife etched into sarcophagus
along with accounts of days
lined up above his linear leather
proclaimed him an accountant of his firm

What ledgers and legal letters, what
meager marks of today will remain,
unsummed and uncollected

Exhibit 5: Catch and Release

To early Americans, being eaten
by coyotes after dying was a cycle
to mark the way out, with no remains
but scat on stone, to plot the story

No need to drag a burden with you
or leave trinkets behind for others
to decipher down the path

This is one way to
take the world with you

Exhibit 6: After Thought

A pair of National Geographic
footprints reveal
the pose of upright man
toed-in the sand

Future abstract progeny will find
our boot prints and think
we had no toes

Ancient graffiti on walls of caves
parallel designs on freeway signs
sprayed with a visual scent
until the can is spent

Someone squats and reads this—
then or now, same message

Exhibit 7: Dress for Success

Brass snaps in an ash tin
from grandfather's overalls
rattle when you shake them
and open the box
then have to cough
inhaling him in

Grandmother stashed with her potash
in a vessel on the top shelf
in the back of the closet
above those dresses no one
can wear and no one
can bear to throw away
yet they will

Exhibit 8: Safekeeping

A spoonful of ashes
in an earthen jar
could well be you
or your dog
in a glass cabinet
with a sign that says
"You *were* what you ate"
and that would be
a wily way to go,
after all.

Worms

1.

Worms come up for old air
during heavy rains and remain
stretched too far to return

Messages bubble up
from the underside of soil
and clay tablets spill ancient
writhings of worms

Above ground, a small child grasps a strip of sidewalk slime
dangles it provocatively over the cavern of her pink mouth
shakes the useless thread, croons to its outstretched band
draws it close to living lips that could revive with warm breath
then, disgusted, hurls it down as worm collapses into mere
reminder of form, an outline of an earth dragon.

2.

"Here lies one whose name was writ on water"
Keats' tombstone reads—the message scrawled
as he gasped his last like a fish rising for old air

They've made worms meat of him
after doing what worms do, lips do
kissing the earth with a pilgrim's kiss

3.

This is what occurs when one cannot speak
the language of the kingdom:

The queen will drink sand from a skull cup
will think of ways to divert herself
as grit settles in her teeth like hopeful seed
(the hourglass leaks somewhere)

Oedipus will solve the riddle of legs
make his twisty brains walk a blind doom
there is comfort in our knowing this is ahead

4.

North American *tumuli*, the mound builders
erected mounds in the shapes of alligators
buffaloes, eagles and serpents
mounds whose interior bones crumbled
into dust when exposed to new air—
so they remain a mystery.

5.

The underworms pulled into their last gasp
have no mouths to kiss pavement, so
form a last line or design, slide
stranded on cement, lost on asphalt
they cannot fathom

Susceptible now to circling birds
to wandering soles
to rubber tires
they are unable to ingest
one last message
to take back to multitudes below
who wait
for news from above
pushing new material
new air
into next time

Estate Sale

If you go into a dead stranger's
house to buy useful items
flagged with price tags
remember—these artifacts
are negotiable: flowered vase,
paste jewelry, jello mold

The Living Room:

Crocheted doilies
pinned where head and hands touched
preserving upholstery past its natural life
so many ceramic figurines
as if life could be still, in one place,
posed just so with
a settee, a fainting chair, a wooden desk
and a bound book of essays

The Study:

Books with that old person smell
hold an invisible mold, a watery dampness
picture frames of accumulated interior scenes
a bowl of fruit gleaming on a table
a lamp throwing a shadow of light

Child-like flat oil paintings of pink desert
narrow forest path with impressionistic pastel
blood sunset in primary colors
frothy ocean shore and distant blues

The frames will be perfect
for your own creative scenes

The Bedroom:

Endless heads with wigs of fake grays
hat boxes poked with hat pins
jewelry boxes with gaudy gold earrings
quilts, crocheted afghans, dolls

The woven comforter
gauze pillows, more doilies
so much latent comfort
and transfiguration in one room

The Kitchen:

Sterling knives, tea cozies
a toaster from the 40s
hand-painted plates of strawberries
divine coasters, dish towels
embroidered with dancing vegetables

Envision the woman's invisible claw still poised
over the china teapot and a sterling
gathering of a lifetime

Outside:

For this sale
you can't take it with you,
though you deeply wish to
for there will always be
at least one more moment to see

May as well
leave it for someone else
to turn over and
haggle the best price
when you turn to go

Top of the Mountain

I.

Overlooking Squaw Valley vistas
and an unnatural turquoise Olympic-sized pool
we lounge poolside sipping iced water
while screams and squawks
of fledgling humans who try too hard
compete with the chirp
of chipmunk,
distant hawk,
wind lyric

Suddenly one chipmunk squeals out
six
        ascending
                chirps

That sound questions like plaintive birds
filmic quips of new-age dinosaurs
or howling air in cavern cracks.
No one seems to listen.

King of the rock, he is upright
alert, drinking air with a purpose
making the noise of a chief
I suck a straw, lifeline
to artificial sustenance
and bubble the bottom of the glass
wanting more of what is not,
watching to see what will happen.
When nothing does.

II.

If I close my eyes I could stray ocean-side
dangling legs over a Pacific Coast precipice
sudden waves breaking shore far below
or I could loll in a Sierra sugar pine tree
needled by the wind, watching osprey stall,
ready to fall for a spawning trout at the alpine lake
in a sieve of green screen, prey to nothing

So why remove myself from paradise so soon?
I would like to say the chipmunk
draws me back to presence
but he doesn't move and
we blend into distraction of a distance.

III.

In another frame, daredevils bungee jump
and leap into a trust of air
for no reason except to feel their hearts
drop to their knees from a skeletal scaffolding.
Designing hieroglyphics of the air,
these gangly, puny spiders without prey
weave nothing that can last in trees
except memory in saying they lasted

I imagine a long, silent swing of my own
in a camping retreat long past
where nine-year-old feet
could just barely sweep
the edge of high pine

Who would have thought
life could wing down to this:

A fake lake resort
walled by concrete stone
and imitation granite
tinged with manicured plants
so perfectly safe,
a far cry from what the
chipmunk remembers.

IV.

And now, the ride to the mountain top
in the cable car, smoother than expected
lends an unnatural way to swing toward
a dalliance with mountain kings

Starting from ski lift base camp
a life line stretches from pole to pole
like a silver necklace with a
dangling diamond carriage
1,800 feet closer to the sun
than the last resort

Inside the glass bauble,
we wobble as sheer cliffs
rush close enough to touch.
Look down if you dare
and you could lose your lunch

At the top, heirs of the mountain
regain power once movement stills,
which justifies terror in the ride
strung with purpose
to reach a zenith

A pinnacle of existence,
just to be able to say later
we were way up there,
shading our eyes to
find the exact spot.

V.

Above, grounded
in a lower world of its own,
but not necessarily a safer one,
the chipmunk, again frozen,
seems to listen for a response
that could not possibly satisfy
what it already must know

For all their awareness,
none of these people
will throw him a peanut.

How to Spot a Serial Killer

He steals blueberries from cornflakes
When you're not looking, at age three

Pulls wings off flies at age four,
Blue bodies writhing

He lights cats on fire at age five
Singed fur stinking

The next thing you know, at six
He cashed his dad's last paycheck

The pup's in the microwave at seven,
And no, it's not dinner

At eight he sneaks ant poison
Into the teacher cup

He trims his mother's toes
At nine with the mower

At ten, the barber scissors
Reach back to their source

At eleven a neighbor girl
Vanishes in a whirl

At twelve, his father is gone
For good in the new cement drive

He's not all that bad
Says his mother

Just harbors a strange way
Of showing affection

His mother is found with
A rope her neck round

Seems as if it all
Comes to a very bad end

Venial Sin

You never returned that library book
Tucked under your arm

The pen that found itself in your pocket
Wasn't yours to pilfer

The candy you snatched from the baby
Stopped your throat

The heart you stole
Bore you down

The lion whose cage you opened
Followed you home and yawned

The mirror borrowed permanently
Slipped and cracked your fate

The word you plagiarized
Lodged in a crevice

No stone to remember by
You forgot too soon

Next time, when you get the urge
Try thieving time and see where it gets

You, hidden under granite
A piece of grit in your tooth

Better to leave the clock alone
With its flailing hands

And try lifting an easier mark
Something that just slipped

Your mind, say a handful
Of rainbow your watch

Threw on the wall
Before it fell

Yellow the Dead Canary

Yellow the dead canary
Upside down dead

Daddy says deep
Dig a hole dark
Lay him in soft

He taps two twigs
Crossed and
Stuck in the dust

Daddy says the
Yellow canary will
Fly to heaven

So I claw the dirt
Each early morning
Eagerly to see

Bedraggled wings
Shriveled claws
Twisted head

He is still there
Stiff, curled dirty yellow
In a shredded tissue bed.

Until one day
I stop digging
And cave in.

Yellow birds
Make me mad.

Yoga at the Y

Human trees emerge
limbs unfurl in homage
to fluorescent sunlight
as trunks lean into Vs
branches bow down to carpet earth while
torsos arc into nether mounds

A voice intones syllables
deep from the diaphragm
head tilted back in calm ecstasy,
hums about energy and inner collection

The voice soothes as bodies shift into shape
flat and still, moving from within as she drones
"You are flexing and relaxing, muscles and bones
so relaxed, more relaxed than sleeping . . . than sleep . . ."

In mirrors to my right
disciples concave into mats
pay homage to the faux earth
and rise and sink softly
fold into paperclip
question mark to mirror

I don't think they can see me in
a reflection outside the moment
as they shoulder rock form,
harden into granite mound,
clasped arms wrap calves
little fetal mounds like that
still as the dead, turning flat

Human twigs soften in the light
a rustle so quiet they must be dreaming of leaves
and I resist the impulse to run out there suddenly
with a scream to wake them all out of their deaths

My own muscles atrophy,
grow immobile
in a stiff wooden chair,
and to move just one hand into word
lips into sound
is a slow wakening

To the Core

Paintings drive by me
In split second review
Oak grove
Farmhouse
Grazing cow family
Irish green pasture
Road like unrolled tires
In rear view
In side view
In windshield
A double sun
Explodes into mirror

This morning splits me open
Like a peach
So sweet
It hurts me
Blind

Passing Time

The crickets sing ching
One long fling
The dogs strike up
A sudden percussion
Of howl and jowl

The night's soft cool breath
Through the window
Tells me that
Another day
Has moved past

Syncopated crickets now
Click out of step
But nicely so
They must have
Shifted the weight
And woo of legs

A German lady told me today
That she was the first one in
Her town to wear shorts
And bear her legs
Forty years ago

That must have been
Some knock-kneed occasion in that
Little town on the Rhine.

Amoura

The candles lit
The roast waits
The china gleams in expectation
You were to arrive at six

My gown rippled smooth
Skin scented in your favorite musk
My muscles ache in desire
You were to arrive at six

The clock chimes six thirty
At least you're not early

The roast pops impatiently
My fingers shake
I finger my glass of wine
And rearrange the roses

You were to arrive at . . .
The doorbell chimes
You come wrapped
In flowers and boxes
And bows on a
Three-piece suit

Come in!
You smell of fresh lime
Your hands warm on mine
The roast waits
The silver shivers

We eat,
Gown in a rumple
Suit on a chair
Candles shine
We sample the fare
The roast awaits
A simpler fate

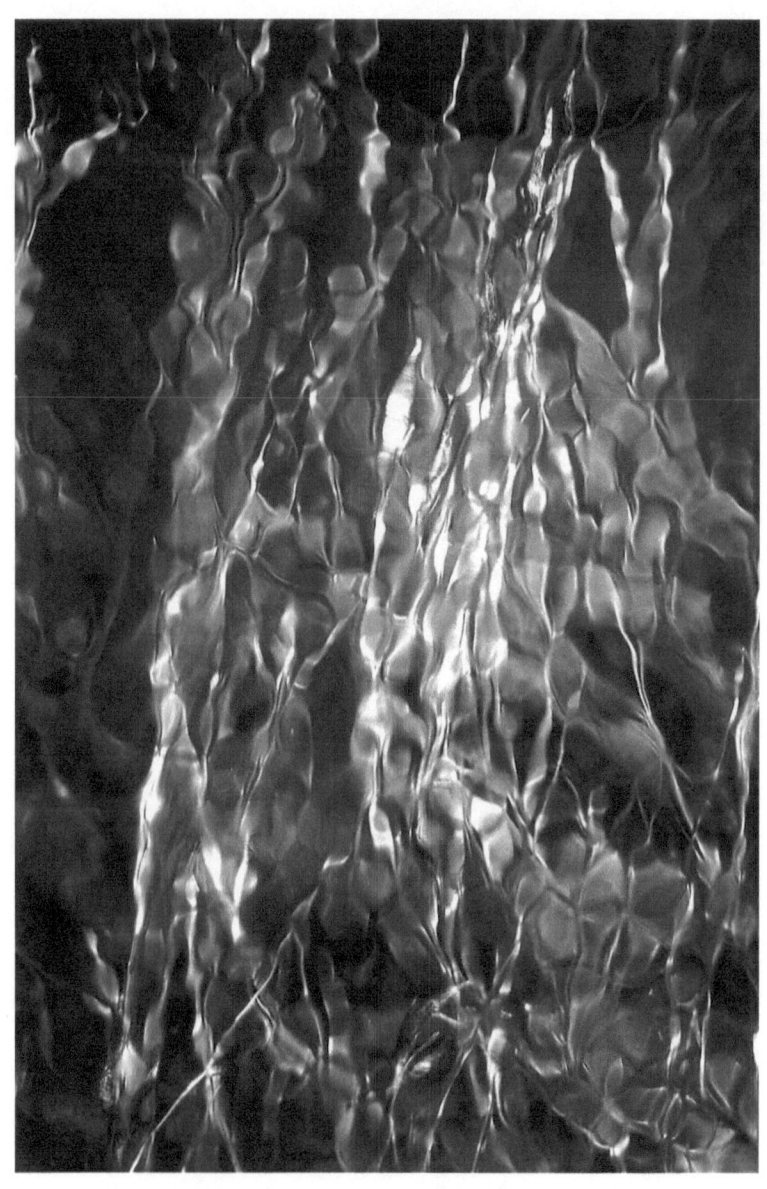

Reeds in Current, Parrotts Ferry, Stanislaus River

VII

Eye for an Eye

*Looking out the window,
one of us witnessed what kept vanishing,
while the other watched what continually emerged.*

—Li-Young Lee

Eye for an Eye

The photographer blinks
An eye in an eye

He will never see
The event in his lens

Locked into now
A flash will illumine

What was then
He was after

But later it is
The photographer who

Misses the moment
Though his eye
Plays upon it still

Milk

A baby cries and my milk still comes
in or so I think after eighteen years
now in a restaurant in the middle of nowhere

My nipples harden in false hope
like an early greening in December
where Mother Lode hills have been gold for months

A grandmother rocks the screams
She pats the baby's back as his lips suck her clothed
shoulder, and I am tables away with imaginary milk

Diners leave in agitation as screams continue
distressed, the infant swims on nerves
his sailor suit bobbing blue, cap bouncing

Grandfather goes on reading his paper, undisturbed
until the baby grabs his glasses and knocks
them to the floor, and he laughs

Do these people know how vital they are at this moment?

The young mother comes back and chubby arms reach out
for her as grandma tries to burp and comfort but
surrenders the baby up to his rightful owner

The bundle still cries and mama can do no better
in this public place with all eyes and all nerves
tight with mother and baby one entity

My breasts tingle and turn into empty bottles
the memory of milk drips
from what once was enough
and now too much

Gift of the Fat Dalmatian

I say *heel* gently
And leash wraps around his neck
Permanent mascara
Rings his eyes

A few random spots
Dot his white skin
Like black blood
Dried fast
To a white rug

The benefactor
Offers food, water
And steak
To his refusal

Shaking in straw
Smooth, pale
He leans his warm side on mine

I own him now
He is my possession
This reverse domino

We bond, and he knows
His place and his weakness

He explores, sniffs, scents,
Then resigns to my will

I can't demand immediate love
Nor command canine affection

Torn from his puppy-hood home
He does not whine
But accepts

I am afraid he is too weak
From years of pedigree

My friendly palm thinks it will
Smooth away sadness
That wrinkles his forehead

Perhaps he will stay when I release
Him from the rope.
Could be a fat chance.

After the Fall

—The Dead Baby

The women sit around the table
A gathering of the goddesses of gloom
Smoking rings around the assembly

Dr. Pepper cans for ashtrays
Oatmeal still crusted
To the empty high chair

A cigarette perched leisurely
On the aluminum edge of a can
Ashes stretching to keep the flame

The line between the fire
And the frost is blue

Blue as the baby's breath
Blue as her bottled eyes
that once held the sky

Blue as her cheeks in a
Squeeze of a drain
Too late

She was only a baby
They shake their heads
Wringing frowns
Into futile furrows

And the ashes continue to fall
Gently like a gray rain
Into a single mound

No one notices
The flame reaching out
To greet the blue

Back to Back

Dark skinny trees
An eagle casts his print in the snow
Wings spread
Snow too cold to melt
Hot wings

White ice
Icicles too cold
To drip

Footprints of wolves
Pack tightly
Night creeps
Eyes dart and slant

Wind rustles the
Moon sneaks up
Eye fastened to a cloud

We prepare for the long night
Straw at our throats
Curved sickle blades gleam

We are
Back to back

Soon they come
One for each
They fly
      Leap
Snarl
      Lunge
Clutch

Teeth tangle in straw
Crescent knife rips the white belly
It opens
Runs red
Fur falls to the side

Next one
Jumps
Again belly slice
Insides open like a mouth.

They rush
Water over stone
Wind on the wheel

Their teeth, needles
In the straw
They scream

Night is over
Clouds slide like
Entrails

Moon sinks into a
Slit of sky

Straw red sunrise
On grey snow
And purple under
The trees

Black skins on the wagon
Wheels spin
A good haul
For the winter

Now home
A deep sleep
And warm meat

Back to back
Man survives.

View of the Garden by a Visitor

The pagurid
Under the squash vine
Could be awaiting an effluent,
Omnipotent coming,
As he crawls.

What is he doing among gourds,
Empty among brimming drinking cups,
Surrounded by homegrown life,
If a pilgrimage indeed awaits?

Does he belong in this homespun
Life of fresh green?
What sustenance, here, monk?

Look at the garden in festival:
The painted cups nod orange red
Color into the wind
The ovular fruits laugh and
Gossip

He hides in his spiral robes
Of the once-predator, unseen
His hermit self retreating
From the corniculate
Fête champêtre

He is the lone-horned misfit
From the grand cornucopia
Creeping out from paradise
With hooded eyes

(How did he ever get here?)
Is he awaiting a baptismal rush,
Blinking in a bare place?
Not a drop.
He claws his way under
Umbrella vines
His chapel chafing clumsily

He is under cover, under shadows
Among the too-green,
Thirsty among laden drinking cups
That are sealed to him.
He is barren among the
Ravages of plenty.

Winding his way
Through tropic undergrowth,
Subsistence slime for him
Was merely misfortune for many.

What satisfying sustenance, this?
That his origin remains banned
From him, his reward?

Sliding alongside the garden hose,
Blind to what it is
Using it as guide
Combing the sidelines,
He scavenges, roots
Finds remnants.

What is he searching for?
His own horn can only
Barely contain him,
Spilling out of itself
In something resembling movement
For movement's sake.

Doesn't he know how
Ridiculous he really is,
This misplaced,
Misshapen
Mandible?

Gold in the Cracks

Face creased in clay
hands scraped by shale
mercury in her blood
the grey lady waits for the gold

Silver poodles at the willows
shell camper docked at the bank
she is locked into a miner sense
and bonded to the elements

Her pan is the sun
when the colors run
a show of yellow marries her
to slow, dull waters

Sluice box steady
rocker willing ready
she sways to the music
of the reedy rusty stream

She bottles flakes, grains, dust,
gold powder and the pebble, but
a rugged, gleaming nugget
lures the sun into her dream

Suction hose homemade
resting in the shade
in the crack that opens
like a track up a withered arm

The river owns her
the willows know her
gold in the cracks
calling lady of the grey

Fingers numb as novocaine
on a tooth won't hold the gold,
her once-lithe limbs now broken
as the river rocks away

But it's anybody's takings
on public free domain
though purse-lipped and forsaken
she grips onto her claim

The cracked old lady
with glitter in her seam
the wracked cold lady
pulled by leaf of precious dream

Stiffens in a silvered pose
fused with pan and plexic hose
she waits for the gold
and waits for the gold.

Parthenogenesis

Snow White virgin of the wild
stretches her limbs
and birds rest, bees hum
in orbits round her head

The goddess gathers and collects
browses, here, there, and selects
through a sieve of the world

She screens and sifts love motes
pausing as if to read random pattern
spread against the semiotic sky

Which animal set off the original explosion?
What birth occurred vicariously
through the senses with
pleasure pulsing in a turgid heart?

Perhaps an ear baby formed,
from waxy fruit of still life
or a nose child who tornadoed into
a dust devil across the winded plain

Did lips blow bubbled abortions
or did the eyes have it, in the tears?

Maybe Eve rubbed Adam the wrong way with that rib.
And didn't Athena spring from her father's crown
fully armed and ready to fight?

If we were once able to produce at will
that might explain why thoughts emerge
suddenly, seeking a place to settle

When did pleasure select love's mansion
in which to pitch a tent in this fashion?

Perhaps the birthing place once lived
in the place of slide
from crown to nave to cave.

Space

A box to the brim
Claims no space within
But it has a place

A space below
Stacks of books
Stretches to the rim

Of the earth and below
An opened hand
Blooms

The outer reaches
Of mind
However blind

Between the eyes
A space disappears
With focus

And though it
Adjoins the
Plane of my face

A blind spot in the
Mirrored highway
Hides it from view

A cluttered desk
No room
For the moon

A place
A space
A face

A zebra at the zoo
Needs more space
Than a wolf

A man measured
In all of this
Needs the world

Harmonica

Forgetting the music
But finding new sound
Here by the river
Where stone shapes the
River songs,
An amulet glitters
In the sand

A talisman lost
By a lover
Maybe last night
Here by the water
Straining under the weight
Of new romance

A four-holed harmonica
On a black string tossed
In a groan
Or a sigh
Flown into sand
Reeds altered by grit

Bitter on the tip
My lips almost envelop
The musical words
Wondering how
The tryst went
How deep
Did it slip
And how the
Taste lingers.

Acknowledgements

I'd like to first of all, thank my creative and wonderful family, my children—Kati, Erika, and Brennan—especially my husband, Gary, for being my rudder and best friend in our journey of love, for going to all the poetry readings, under mock protest at times. Much gratitude to my parents, Otto and Magdalena, for love and goodness, and to my sister, Lili, close to my heart, and her family.

I want to thank all my Writers Unlimited friends who read some of these poems, including Jackie Richmond, Glenn Wasson, Dave Self, Ted Laskin, Linda Field, Joy Roberts, Antoinette May, Lou Gonzalez, Jennifer Tristano, Jim Lanier, Jackie Rogers, and Shanda McGrew. My thanks also to Manzanita Writers Press staff for their artistic nourishment. Many laughs go to Joyce Dedini—one fantastic layout designer—my good friend, who is patient yet firm with me. I would like to thank Ron Pickup for all his help, our poetic friendship, and his stunning photography. My gratitude to poet Dennis Schmitz, who taught me to seek the poem outside the poem.

About the Poet

Monika Rose, of Calaveras County, California, edits *Manzanita: Poetry and Prose of the Mother Lode and Sierra*, and has been published in *Tule Review, Rattlesnake Review, Poetry Now, Mindprint Review, Squaw Valley Review, The Journal, Refrigerate After Opening, Mokehelion Review*, and others. Her work appears in *Shadows of Light*, an anthology of poetry and photography of the Sierra. She is currently writing a novel based on her parents' WWII experiences told through an immigrant daughter's eyes, and is working on a literary thriller—a novel involving surveillance, privacy, and voyeuristic obsession.

www.ingramcontent.com/pod-product-compliance
Lightning Source LLC
Chambersburg PA
CBHW030324100526
44592CB00010B/565

Lizard

I.

    I am ready for the solitude
    the peace of the forest
    I, alone,
    on a rock.

    Bring back my lizard self,
    unwinking
    in this world of move.

    My stillness is also
    the rock against the wind
    flung in abandon.

    I land, now,
    a rock.

    I could become
    a bird.

II.

    Giving myself to
    the stone
    I am a lost lizard

    The blink becomes
    a forgotten art.

    My tail moves round
    the circle
    of still.

What shakes the eye but the invisible?

—Theodore Roethke

Previously Published

The poet acknowledges the publications in which poems have appeared:

Carp - *Mindprint Review; Shadows of Light*
Battered Woman - *Mindprint Review*
Eye - *Mindprint Review*
A Poet - *Mindprint Review; The Journal*
What is to Wilderness - *Tule Review*
Variations on a Skipping Stone - *Medussa's Kitchen*
Bull Pine in the Window - *Squaw Review*
Love and Finance - *Calaveras Enterprise; Poetry Now; Medussa's Kitchen*
Beauty and the Beast - *B.L. Kennedy Interview series; Rattlesnake Review*
Cleaning Fish - *Rattlesnake Review; B.L. Kennedy Interview series*
Drop of Moon - *Refrigerate After Opening*
Chester and the Bluebird - *Mokhelion Review*
Deer in the Road - *Mokhelion Review*
Estate Sale - *Poets Corner Press*
Amoura - *Calaveras Enterprise*
Fragment - *Refrigerate After Opening*
Nails - *Manzanita*
Bull Pine - *Manzanita*
Marimba Mountains - *Wild Edges*
View of the Garden by a Visitor - *The Journal*
Gold in the Cracks - *The Journal*
There is a Cough - *The Journal*
Black Dog - *Manzanita*
Lizard - *Manzanita*
Back to Back - *The Journal*
Alignment - *Poetry Now*